Successful Appraisals in a week

DI KAMP

Successful
Appraisals
in a week

DI KAMP

Hodder & Stoughton

A MEMBER OF THE HODDER HEADLINE GROUP

Orders: please contact Bookpoint Ltd, 39 Milton Park, Abingdon, Oxon
OX14 4TD. Telephone: (44) 01235 400414, Fax: (44) 01235 400454. Lines are
open from 9.00 – 6.00, Monday to Saturday, with a 24 hour message
answering service. Email address: orders@bookpoint.co.uk

British Library Cataloguing in Publication Data

A catalogue for this title is available from
the British Library

ISBN 0 340 71205 8

First published 1994
Second edition 1998
Impression number 10 9   8 7   6 5 4 3 2 1
Year   2002   2001   2000 1999 1998

Typeset by Multiplex Techniques Ltd, St Mary Cray, Kent.
Printed for Hodder & Stoughton Educational, a division of Hodder
Headline Plc, 338 Euston Road, London NW1 3BH by Cox and Wyman Ltd.,
Reading, Berkshire.

the *Institute*
of *Management*

FOUNDATION

The Institute of Management (IM) exists to promote the development, exercise and recognition of professional management. The Institute embraces all levels of management from student to chief executive and supports its own Foundation which provides a unique portfolio of services for all managers, enabling them to develop skills and achieve management excellence.

For information on the various levels and benefits of membership, please contact:

Department HS
Institute of Management
Cottingham Road
Corby
Northants NN17 1TT

Tel: 01536 204222
Fax: 01536 201651

This series is commissioned by the Institute of Management Foundation.

C O N T E N T S

Appraisal systems are now in operation in many organisations, yet they are still often regarded as someone else's bright idea, or as 'flavour of the month', with little relevance to everyday working practice.

To many of us, appraisal means extra paperwork, trying to find something positive to say to someone, and listening to their complaints.

We wonder how tactful we need to be about someone's poor performance and we wonder what on earth we're supposed to say if someone does their job well.

If appraisals are linked by our company to performance-related pay, or promotion prospects, then that gives them a little more meaning; except that we already know who we think is good and who needs sorting out!

The potential usefulness of appraisals is frequently lost in the apparent artificiality of the interview, and its isolation from everyday performance management.

It is worth re-examining how we put appraisals into practice, so as to turn them into the useful tool they are intended to be for us as managers.

When implemented well, appraisals are a vital component of the healthy development of both individuals and the organisation.

Some simple guidelines, reminders and checks will help us to use them as a positive contribution to the life of the organisation.

Preparation
- define the purpose and benefits of appraisal
- set the appraisal framework, linked to organisational and individual goals
- establish and agree the procedures and responsibilities for the appraisal interview
- establish a process for the appraisal interview

Implementation
- clarify your own role as appraiser
- use the interview to recognise achievement and progress
- work out with the individual ways of dealing constructively with areas for improvement
- make goals and targets clear and specific

Follow-up
- ensure that there is a continuing support system for performance management and development

Over the week, we will look at how to put these guidelines into practice.

Setting the context: why appraise?

Today we will set the context for applying appraisal skills effectively.

The context

- purpose of appraisal systems
- benefits to organisation
- benefits to the individual
- benefits to the manager
- principles of appraisal

If we don't know what can be gained from effective appraisal then we have no reason to view it as a positive and useful activity.

Often, it turns into a yearly 'chat' with the individual where neither side is sure what will come out of it.

As manager, you know that you're supposed to sound positive, no matter what. Yet most of those we will be appraising are neither 'stars' nor awful at what they do. What can you say when someone just does their job well? And what do you say when someone is not doing well and you are supposed to sound positive?

It is hard to give direction to the appraisal without a clear purpose, and the manager can feel solely responsible for trying to 'make it work'.

The individual being appraised, on the other hand, may fear that if they say the 'wrong thing', they will ruin any chances of promotion.

If you are using 360° feedback, they may also fear the effect of negative responses from others and wonder how to offset that effect.

It is important to be clear about how appraisals can contribute to organisational effectiveness, so that both sides use the opportunity well.

To achieve this clarity, we need to look at the purpose of having an appraisal system, and identify how it can benefit those involved.

The purpose of appraisal

Appraisal means many different things in different contexts. Usually, in a work context, it implies some type of formal, recorded interview with every member of staff at regular intervals, e.g. yearly, and often seems to be isolated from the rest of the everyday contact between managers and their staff.

For us to use appraisal effectively, we need to see it as part of overall performance management and development.

We all like to know how we're doing as individuals, and organisations need to know how they match up to their goals and targets.

Often this is monitored in an informal way. After all, we're all very good at noticing if something isn't going according to plan, or isn't as good as we want it to be.

However, this informal monitoring tends to ignore the genuine progress and achievement that takes place.

We tend to assume that if no one says anything is wrong, then we're probably doing reasonably well! In organisational terms, this can be translated into: if we're still making a profit, we're doing OK.

Appraisal is designed as a means of monitoring the progress and achievement of the organisation, to encourage and support the continuing development of that organisation in a changing world.

This not only helps the organisation as a whole to continue to work towards optimum effectiveness, but also provides departments and individuals within that organisation with a clear overall development plan, into which their own development plans can fit.

For example, it will make far more sense to me that I should learn to use a computerised database if it is introduced into the organisation with clear explanations of how it will contribute to the increased effectiveness of the organisation.

If it seems that the computer has been introduced just because there was some money spare in the annual budget, I am more likely to defend the old system, and resent the time I have to spend on the change.

Appraisal is also designed to encourage and motivate employees continually to develop their skills, so that they are of ever-increasing value to their organisation.

We will increase this motivation if we offer positive recognition of progress and achievement, as well as support and help in developing in those areas that are seen to be weaker.

Appraisals give us the opportunity to give this recognition, and to identify with someone how they could improve in areas where they are weaker.

So both the individual and the organisation gain from the process.

Here is a checklist of the purposes of appraisal:

The purposes of appraisal

- to monitor the progress and achievement of the organisation as a whole
- to encourage and support the continuing development of that organisation in a changing world
- to encourage and motivate employees continually to develop their skills, so that they are of ever-increasing value to their organisation

The benefits of effective appraisal

To ensure that appraisal is used well, rather than just paid lip-service to, it is important that the benefits to all those involved are recognised and spelt out.

We all need to feel that the process will have a pay-off for us personally. Then we will be prepared to invest some time and energy in it.

We also need to feel that it has some relevance, both short-term and long-term, to our professional and business development.

When we put into practice the principles and processes of appraisal effectively, then there is positive benefit and development for the appraiser, for the individual being appraised and for the organisation.

It becomes a welcome and useful part of the employee's working life. It is also a vital part of the manager's role, both in offering support to his/her staff, and in maintaining the development of the organisation. As managers, we need to be aware of the benefits and be able to state them to others, to make sure that appraisal is treated as something which has a valuable contribution to make to working life.

Benefits for the organisation
Organisations as a whole will gain from effective appraisals:

- by having motivated employees
- by learning what skills are available which can be drawn on to enhance their overall performance
- by being able to identify, before a problem arises, how they may need to train or develop their employees to meet organisational goals
- by having their finger on the pulse of the internal set-up

Benefits for the individual
What of the person being appraised? For the individual, appraisal provides an opportunity to:

- receive recognition and support from management, as they develop in the work role
- be reminded of how they are contributing to the effectiveness of the organisation overall
- voice their views and offer constructive suggestions on both their own development and that of the overall organisation

Benefits for the manager
For the manager, the appraisal is an opportunity to:

- enhance the relationship with the individual
- give the individual recognition and support in their continuing development
- enhance the individual's motivation by reminding them of the overall context of organisational goals to which they are contributing
- evaluate the effectiveness of individual contributions to the overall effectiveness of the organisation
- gather information which may help to develop further ways of enhancing organisational effectiveness

Principles of appraisal

So how do we turn the appraisal into this positive and useful tool?

Whether we are appraising on an informal or formal basis, there are guidelines to the approach to take which will make it far more likely that the appraisal has the effect we want.

The principles of appraisal provide a framework to define the approach, so that we undertake the appraisal with a clear idea of our intentions and purpose.

The overriding principle of appraising is that we encourage the person being appraised to take on more and more responsibility for his/her own development.

In doing this, we need to remember that the individual will have some feeling of *not* being in control, at least initially.

Most times, an appraisal is imposed on us; but even if we have actively asked for it, we tend to do so because we don't feel that we can sort out any problems or a schedule for development ourselves.

We also need to remember that the individual knows more about their own achievement, progress, and problems than anyone else – they experience it, as opposed to observing it!

So our intention in appraisal is to enable the individual to take more and more of an active part in identifying their own strengths and weaknesses, and in deciding what to do about it.

An appraisal is an interaction between two people
In other words, the appraisee is human too and so, we need

to ensure that we treat them with respect, in order to build up trust.

If they do not feel that they can trust the manager, then the contribution they make will be limited, and the usefulness of the appraisal reduced.

If we do not come across as 'human', and accepting of them, then they will be intimidated, and if they feel that we may use what they say against them in some way, then they will say as little as possible about any difficulties and problems they may have. As we all know, these will then show up at the most inopportune time, and cause us bigger problems because they affect the appraisee's work.

Appraisals should have a positive intention and outcome
This requires that we set a positive tone to the whole appraisal. Positive recognition is important to all of us. We

like it when someone says thank you, or remarks on something we've achieved or progressed in. We can offer this recognition in the appraisal, and thereby encourage the individual.

We also know that building on strengths is easier than putting the emphasis on correcting weaknesses.

Finally, we want to ensure that any weak areas are dealt with, so we need to offer constructive help to the individual in finding a way to improve performance. After all, being told that we were not doing well enough at something never helped us to do it better – it only made us feel worse.

The principles of appraisal checklist
- The individual will take more and more responsibility for their own development and we will help them to do that
- We will establish trust and a good relationship as the basis for the appraisal
- An appraisal has a positive intention and outcome, and we will use it to help the individual to use their strengths well and identify ways of improving their performance

The role of the manager in appraisals
Having looked at the purpose and benefits of appraisals, we can begin to identify the first stages of how we can ensure that appraisals are useful and constructive.

It is up to us, as managers, to set the context for the appraisal, and educate our staff into viewing it as useful. We also need to remind ourselves of the potential of appraisal, so that we treat it as an important part of our responsibilities, and prepare for it properly.

We are responsible for setting the tone which will help our staff to treat appraisal as a useful and constructive part of their overall development. This is especially important when appraisal has not been seen in this light before.

By thinking through our own way of expressing the benefits, purpose and intention of appraisal, we will already have begun the journey towards more successful appraisal.

Setting the context

Let's conclude with a reminder of what we need to do to set the right context for appraisal.

1 Establish the purpose of the appraisal, the intended outcomes and the approach.
2 Explain the purpose, outcomes and approach to our staff, and agree these with them.
3 Encourage the person being appraised to contribute actively to their own appraisal.
4 Give recognition to progress and achievement.
5 Help find ways to overcome obstacles to progress.
6 Ensure that we use the information which we find out in appraisals with integrity, to help the individual to progress.
7 Remind ourselves of the potential value of appraisals, if conducted well.

Formulating an effective appraisal

Today we will clarify what exactly is being appraised and why.

Framework for appraisal

- making it relevant
- making it meaningful
- making it comprehensive
- making it developmental

If we are going to conduct effective appraisals, we need to ensure that both sides are clear about what exactly is being appraised.

Of course we all know that we appraise performance, but we so often don't know exactly what that means in practice.

So we pick up on what we *have* noticed. This tends to be either outstanding performance or poor performance in a particular area or activity which happened recently.

This simply leaves our employee confused about what's important: 'Was my obvious lack of interest at the last staff meeting more important than consistently meeting my sales targets?'

Alternatively, if there is nothing which we have noticed, we tend to make vague and general statements which closely resemble old-style school reports: 'Your work is generally fairly good, and you continue to make progress.'

Our employee is left with no clear picture of what we mean – probably because we don't know what we mean!

Even worse, we may then go on to ask them what they think. How can they comment when they don't know what we are looking at in their performance?

We need to make explicit, for ourselves and for those we appraise, what areas of performance are being considered.

Formulating relevant appraisals

The first step in establishing what to appraise with an individual is to check what the organisation as a whole is aiming towards.

Your organisation's mission statement, or the company's aims and objectives will tell you this.

We need to frame what we are appraising in the larger context of what the organisation has as its goals, so that it is seen as relevant, both for the organisation, and for the employee.

For example, suppose your company has, as part of its mission statement, 'putting customers first'. It will be important to look at how your staff deal with customers as part of their appraisal.

You may also have specific departmental goals, which are derived from the overall goals of the organisation. For example, suppose your department has as one of its goals 'reduction of customer complaints'. It will be important to look at how your staff contribute to reducing customer complaints.

Putting appraisals in an organisational framework

1 What is your organisation's mission statement?
2 What areas of skill, behaviour, or attitude does it imply for employees?
3 What are your department's goals?
4 What areas of skill, behaviour, or attitude do they imply for employees?

Answering these questions will give us the first part of a framework for appraisal.

These areas of performance will be relevant to your organisation, because the appraisal will show how the individual is contributing to the organisational goals.

They will also make sense to the individual, by relating their individual achievements to what the organisation as a whole wishes to achieve.

Formulating a meaningful appraisal

The next step in establishing what to appraise with an individual is to ensure that what is appraised relates to their job specification.

If my duties and responsibilities include the management of an administrative records system, but my manager never refers to that in my appraisal, I may begin to wonder if the appraisal has anything to do with my real job – or whether that was an important responsibility after all!

Look at your employee's original job description and specification. (If this does not exist, ask them to help you to compile a list of main duties, responsibilities and requirements.)

5 Identify from this the main areas of performance to be appraised.
6 What skills, behaviours or attitudes are required to fulfil this job specification?

We now have the basis for a relevant and meaningful framework for appraisal.

Your answers to questions 2, 4, 5 and 6 above will identify for you the main criteria of a competent performance in this role.

You can use information from an appraisal based on these criteria to demonstrate how that person contributes to organisational and departmental goals.

The criteria are relevant and meaningful to the person being appraised, because they can be shown to be related directly to the organisation's goals, and to their own job specification.

A comprehensive appraisal framework

So far, we have looked at how to link the appraisal criteria to both the organisational goals and the individual role. This ensures that the appraisal will have some relevance and meaning by making its links to the work context explicit. However, it is still easy to miss information or acknowledgement of an individual's progress or achievement.

More and more organisations are now acknowledging the importance of the individual's continuing personal and professional development. We live in a world where change has become the norm. We need individuals who show initiative, who are willing to learn, who are flexible.

It is therefore important that we have, within the appraisal framework, some means of identifying personal and professional achievements which are not strictly related to the narrow work context. They may, however, be evidence of an individual's developmental capacity.

For example, do you know if any of your staff:

- Work as a volunteer in their community?
- Run a Scout group?
- Are on the PTA for a local school?
- Are taking an Open College course or evening class?
- Are expert at climbing or orienteering?
- Have recently learnt to sail, or speak a foreign language, or do karate?

These and many other out-of-work activities demonstrate that the person has talents and abilities which could well be transferred to the work context in some way.

They also demonstrate willingness to learn, and to be involved – vital requisites in a changing organisation.

Most organisations have some form of training and development programme for their staff. However, as managers, we do not always pick up on what courses or seminars our staff have attended, and what they may have gained from it.

This is particularly true of training in so-called 'soft skills', those areas which are not directly related to specific knowledge or technical skill development.

The appraisal framework needs to pick up on any professional development that the appraisee has undertaken.

Finally, there is an area of performance appraisal which is often missed because it is hard to define. This is what we are like as a person to work with. Remember the stereotype of the doctor's receptionist as a 'dragon'? And the 'ordinary' person in the office who always makes everyone feel comfortable, and is liked by everyone?

There are people in organisations who fulfil their job specifications exactly, yet are uncooperative or even hostile with others. And there are those who do nothing extraordinary in their actual work role, yet help to create and maintain an excellent team atmosphere.

It is important that we notice and value how people are with others, and how that contributes to the effectiveness of the organisation.

Using feedback from peers, subordinates and customers can significantly add to our awareness of how someone works with others. Encouraging the appraisee to ask others for their opinion of their behaviour and attitudes under questions 2, 4 and 6, will add to the information about personal qualities.

7 What activities or courses are your staff involved in, outside work?

8 What training or development have your staff undertaken, and how did it affect them?

9 What are the personal qualities required of your staff?

Looking for development

In business these days, continuous improvement is a vital theme, both organisationally and individually. An appraisal system is intended to encourage the development of the individual.

We must ensure that the appraisal framework identifies and recognises the employee's development. After all, if I have been doing this job for years I may be competent at it, yet make no effort to take it any further.

To some extent, the questions already identified will pull this out. To ensure that we have really identified development, we need some 'markers'.

At each appraisal we need to know how the person was performing at their last appraisal (or, if it's an initial appraisal, what their starting point is).

Then we need to assess with them how they have improved on that performance.

Finally, we need to agree with them how they will continue to improve their performance.

What often happens is that we only pick up on a need to improve where performance is poor. For example, if someone is lax with their record-keeping, we ask them to 'get better at it'. If their work is already competent, we tend to just make lame statements like, 'Well done, keep up the good work.' This tends to bring two unwanted results:

- their work standard actually deteriorates as they 'sit back on their laurels'
- they are less motivated because there is nothing in particular to aim for

The alternative is to ask them to identify how they could improve their performance even more, and to encourage them to continue to develop their skills to do so.

10 How are your staff demonstrating continuous development?

11 What areas could you look at with them for further development?

12 What support and help is available to make these developments?

Using the framework for appraisal

We can use this framework in two different ways, depending on what already exists as an appraisal system.

If you haven't already developed a formal written procedure for appraising, you can use the questions asked throughout this chapter to construct an appraisal format and recording framework.

The example below shows how these questions could be used as the basis for guiding both the appraiser and the appraisee in what to look for in an appraisal, and what to 'collect' as evidence.

Example

1 This company's mission statement implies that employees should demonstrate flexibility, a high standard of customer service and a willingness to develop their skills.
   How have you (has this employee) demonstrated this?
2 This department's goals are to reduce customer complaints and to increase the speed of delivery of service.
   How have you (has this employee) contributed to these goals?
3 Your main duties are: reception of visitors; answering telephone queries; processing of repairs procedures; maintaining the records of customer usage.
   What are your (are your employee's) examples of best practice in this, and what exactly did you do?
   What do you feel you (they) could improve on in your job performance, and how could you achieve that?

4 What are you (is your employee) involved in outside work, which you feel demonstrates skills/abilities/ potential which are important to you and/or your organisation?

5 What training and/or development activities have you (has your employee) undertaken?
   How have they been useful to you, personally or professionally?

6 What personal qualities do you have (has your employee got) which you feel contribute to your (employee's) value in this organisation?
   Give an example (examples) of how they have been used.

7 How are you (is your employee) developing your own work performance?

8 How else would you like to develop your work performance?

Notice how this set of questions makes clear what the areas for appraisal are. It ensures that all parties to the appraisal are working to the same criteria, and that those criteria are relevant to the organisation and the individuals.

You can also use this framework to help those involved in appraisal to make the process meaningful.

You may already have a recording system for appraisal which asks general questions, or has general headings.

Example
1 Achievements over the last year
2 Targets met
3 Areas for improvement
4 Agreed new targets

It may then be useful to use the questions above to help both parties prepare for the appraisal by using them as guidelines to what to discuss, in order to identify what to record in the different sections.

We have been looking at a major area of preparation for successful appraisals. When you first decide on this form of preparation, it may seem daunting. However, once you have done it, you will see clear benefits:

- it enables you to tie in appraisals to business objectives
- it enables you to make appraisals more meaningful to those being appraised
- it makes appraisals useful to you as a manager, by giving you evidence of how you and your employees are contributing to the business and what else you need to do
- it enables you to have a clear focus in appraisals, rather than wondering what to discuss
- it enables those being appraised to come prepared with specific evidence, and ideas for targets

Obviously you may wish to use a slightly different format to develop your own criteria or framework for appraisal. What matters is that you stop and clarify what exactly you are appraising when you appraise 'performance'. By agreeing the criteria explicitly with your employees, you have already improved the value and usefulness of appraisals in your organisation.

The appraiser's role, I: setting the framework

Today we are going to begin to look at what exactly your role should be as an appraiser, if you want to appraise successfully.

Up to now, we have been looking at the general preparation which needs to be done for setting up successful appraisals. Having laid these foundations, we now need to examine your role as appraiser in:

- clarifying the basis for appraisal
- agreeing procedures for appraisal
- agreeing responsibilities for appraisal
- preparing for appraisal

Clarifying the basis for appraisal

It is not enough to sort out for yourself what the purpose of appraisal is, and what criteria you will use.

We have all been in the situation where the other person thought it was obvious why something was important, but we didn't grasp it at all. In that situation, we just feel frustrated and confused.

So don't take it for granted that the person being appraised will see appraisals as valuable, or that they will understand the framework of criteria you are using. The basic rule is: *explain and make explicit.*

This will make your life easier, because it will ensure that you are both 'singing from the same hymn sheet'. It will also enable the person being appraised to come prepared with relevant information, examples and ideas.

So how do you start?

First of all, you need to spell out the purpose of the appraisal.

Example
'Appraisals are intended to monitor your (the employee's) performance at work in a constructive way.

They provide an opportunity:

- to review what you have been doing, and how you have been doing it
- to discuss any issues you have which you think may be slowing down your progress, and find ways of dealing with them

They give you (the employee) the opportunity to:

- give evidence of your achievements and progress, and receive recognition and support for these
- be reminded of how you are contributing to the effectiveness of the whole organisation
- voice your views and offer constructive suggestions on both your own development and that of the organisation

Finally, in the appraisal, we can agree together what goals for development you are going to set yourself for the next appraisal, and how they can be achieved.'

You could adapt this to your own style, and perhaps even produce it as a written document, to give to the individual as reinforcement after you have read it out, and checked it through with them.

Next, you need to emphasise the principles of the appraisal, and the way in which it will be handled. Remember that most people have a negative experience of performance reviews. From school-days onwards, when someone 'in authority' has commented on their work, it has generally been to judge and criticise them.

So you need to state clearly and explicitly that an appraisal:

- is a two-way process
- is intended to be useful and constructive
- will recognise positively what the person has achieved
- will help to identify how that person can develop further

You should also point out clearly that their involvement and contributions are vital to the success of the appraisal.

Third, you need to make explicit what is being appraised and why. The guidelines in the previous chapter will help you and them to understand this.

Finally, they need to be clear that feedback from others is for them to use as part of their evidence on their performance, and that this information will help both of you to identify achievements as well as areas for development. Its purpose is to enhance the information available, not to criticise them.

It will take a little time to make sure that these foundations for a successful appraisal are understood and agreed with the person being appraised. This time is well spent, as it is fulfilling a part of your role as appraiser. You are giving the individual the information they need to take an active and constructive part in the appraisal process. By empowering them in this way, you are laying the groundwork to make the appraisal itself more focused, purposeful and productive.

Agreeing procedures and responsibilities for appraisal

Having clarified the general principles we will be working to in appraisal, we now need to make clear the procedures for appraisal.

1 Setting a time for the appraisal interview
To reinforce the statement that appraisals are important and useful, we need to demonstrate that we take them seriously by the way we set them up.

a The interviews are given a definite time slot in the diary

Most appraisal interviews are held at six-monthly or yearly intervals. They therefore have a lot of ground to cover, and require about two hours to be useful. This time needs to be clearly allocated.

b The time fixed for the appraisal interview is given priority in the diaries of both parties

It is no good saying that your employee must keep this date and time clear if you then cancel because you have an urgent report to write!

As managers, we must set the example of treating appraisals as an important part of our business by keeping to the set time unless we are really forced to change it. Appraisal intervals cannot just be 'fitted in' if they are to be taken seriously.

It may be worth setting aside a set period in the week or month just for appraisal interviews, so that they become a fixture in your calendar.

c   We need to fix the time well enough in advance to give our employees time to prepare properly for the interview

We want our employees to come to the interview well prepared. That means that they need time to review their own performance, and think about their evidence and examples.

If we only give them a day's notice, we are implying that their own review is not that important – assuming they are busy in their job role.

Sometimes, the dates for appraisals are set months in advance. In this case, it is useful to remind your employee a couple of weeks before the date, so that they remember to do their preparation – and likewise yourself.

2 *Agreeing what preparation the appraisee needs to do*

There are several approaches we can take to supporting the person being appraised in their preparation. It is not enough to give them time and prior warning. They also need some guidelines as to what you mean by preparation.

It can be useful to ask them to make notes, and to offer them a recording sheet which prompts useful evidence and ideas. If you use a recording sheet, it is important that you make clear to them that it is for *their* benefit and use, not for your records.

Otherwise, a preparation checklist can be useful, leaving them to make notes in their own way.

Before you ask them to record anything, it is important to restate what exactly you want from them. You may choose to use your own version of the following:

Purpose of record

1 To gather evidence to present at appraisal:
   a of own achievements on targets agreed last time
   b of own progress on targets agreed last time
   c of own achievement and progress on other steps
      towards the goal(s)
2 To remind yourself of any problems you encountered,
   why you think the problems occurred, and any solutions
   to the problems which you thought of and/or applied.
3 To remind yourself of areas:
   a in which you would benefit from more training
   b in which you would benefit from further practice
   c you would like to pursue further
   d on which you would like to concentrate
4 To remind yourself of anything which felt really good –
   where you felt pleased with your own learning, or
   where you felt that the methods used to help you learn
   were particularly effective.
5 To note anything else you might want to say at
   appraisal.
   *This record is your personal record of your progress
   towards your goals.*
   It is an 'aide-memoire' to help you to contribute as
   effectively as possible towards your own appraisal.

Without the reminder, you may well forget what you
wanted to say, particularly if your appraiser is more
confident than you in the process.

But *you* know more than anyone else about your own
progress – so don't miss the chance to use that
information.

If you would like to give them a recording sheet to use, something like the following can be useful:

Record for appraisee

Tasks done (to remind you of what you've been working on)

Training/teaching received (to remind you of what you've been offered help in, by whom, and how useful it was)

Steps towards goals achieved since last appraised

Steps towards goals made progress in (refer to your copy of the last appraisal record to identify relevant areas)

Areas where problems arose (suggest solutions as well if possible)

Areas you would like to work on next (may be for any of the reasons listed in purpose of recording)

Other comments (anything you would like to say about your progress generally)

Extra suggestions for preparation which you can make are:

1 That they bring with them supporting evidence e.g. the first set of minutes they've ever written, a letter from a customer they found difficult to deal with, the end-of-module comments from their college tutor, etc.
   This will give you the opportunity to give specific acknowledgement on things in which they have done well.

It will also mean that you can discuss specifically with them areas they are finding difficult.

2 That they ask for feedback on their performance from others – colleagues, other managers, customers, trainers.

Often we don't know what others think of our performance, and their viewpoint can be very useful information.

Do stress that this is for *their* information, and it is up to them to use it constructively.

This may seem like an awful lot to get across to someone, 'just for an appraisal'.

It is worth noticing that:

1 It is only the first time that it takes a long time – after that, you just need to remind them.

Most people will respond very positively to such clear guidelines, and will take on responsibility for preparing thereafter, because they see how useful it is to them.

2 You are empowering the person being appraised to take responsibility for making the appraisal useful and focused.

3 The act of preparing is in itself a development exercise. It is teaching the individual to review their own performance, to learn from that, and to identify how they could improve.

4 The preparing will help the individual to be realistic about the appraisal. They will come to the interview confident of their own ability and progress and/or aware of their need to improve and in what areas.

Explaining and actioning your preparation

If, as managers, we go through the preparatory work with the person being appraised, we have made our own preparation for the actual appraisal interview much easier.

However, some preparation still remains to be done.

a   Read through the previous appraisal record

This will remind us of the targets we agreed with the individual and the areas in which they had progressed at their last review.

b   Gather information from other sources

There may be obvious points we need to follow up on: Did they complete that training programme? How did that project go?

It is useful and constructive to find out factual information before the interview.

If you have not asked the appraisee to get feedback from others, you may wish to consult with their peers, subordinates and customers.

Be careful how you ask about their performance, to elicit clear and specific information.

Examples of useful questions:

1 Jack wanted to develop his skills in . . . In what ways do you think he is progressing? Are there any ways that you think his development could be increased?
2 Can you give me any examples where Jill has shown good progress whilst doing . . . ? Can you give me any

areas where you think she could progress more quickly by approaching it a different way?

3 If I ask you to summarise Jack's progress over the last month in relation to his goals, what would you say?

NB It is important to remind people of what the criteria for development are: Jack may be pleasant to work with, but may not have improved his carpentry skills at all.

c Consider your own view of their performance and collect your own evidence

You can use the same checklist as they use, and can also make brief notes throughout the year of things you notice, so that the information is already there. This helps us to consider the whole period, rather than just focusing on something that happened last week.

d Clarify for yourself what results you want from this appraisal

This will remind you to:

- apply the principles of appraisal
- refer to the business goals and refresh your awareness of them
- refer to their job specification
- focus your attention on learning and development rather than faults

It is important that you tell the person being appraised that you are doing this preparation.

They will then know that you are taking the appraisal seriously. They will also know that you will have a great deal of information on them to hand, which will encourage them to make more effort to gather relevant information also.

Finally, it is important to timetable yourself the space to do this preparation. You can use the same device you used for the person being appraised to prompt you into allocating specific time for information-gathering.

Explaining how the interview will proceed
We all tend to get rather nervous about 'interviews', however well we know and get on with the interviewer. It is made easier if we know beforehand the structure of the interview, and the approach to be used. We will discuss this in detail in later chapters.

You need to clarify your approach and the structure you will use, and then ensure that you explain this to the person being appraised beforehand.

To a large extent, this is implicit in all the explanations you have given them so far. It is, however, still worth making explicit, so that you are sure that they really do understand how the interview will be run.

So far we have explored in some detail all the preparatory stages for an appraisal.

Remember: time spent on preparation saves time in the long run, and makes the time spent on the appraisal much more valuable and focused.

The appraiser's role, II: attitudes and approaches

Today we will look at the role of the appraiser in terms of the attitude and approach needed to result in successful appraisals – the 'how to be an appraiser' when conducting the appraisal interviews.

Key ideas are:

- being ready
- establishing trust
- empowering
- finding out
- listening
- negotiating
- agreeing

Being ready

We often find that we come into another meeting carrying with us the pressures of previous and following activities. Although we intend to give the meeting our full attention, the fact is that our minds are elsewhere.

It only takes a few minutes to set your 'baggage' aside, relax, and focus on the meeting you are about to go into. This will help you to pay full attention in the way in which the person being appraised deserves.

We also need to realise that, as appraiser, you can feel as tense and nervous about the interview as the person being appraised. You want it to go well, and be useful, but you may be new to the role, or you may be unsure about your credibility as an appraiser.

If this is the case, remember the following:

- this is not a test for either side, it's a joint venture, with both of you wanting it to be useful
- the person being appraised will be more nervous than you; concentrate on making them feel all right, and you will automatically ease down yourself
- take a few deep breaths before you start, and consciously relax muscular tension; if you can physically relax, you will be more able to perform well
- if you admit to being a bit nervous about it to the person being appraised, they will think more of you, not less; it makes them feel less 'unique' in being nervous, it establishes something in common, and it means that they will understand if you want to rephrase a question or correct some statement that you feel isn't quite 'in the right spirit'

Do glance at your preparation notes just to remind yourself of your focus.

Checklist for being ready
- take a few minutes to separate yourself from previous activities and ones which you have to do afterwards
- take a couple of deep breaths and relax
- glance at your preparation notes

Establishing trust

We need to ensure that the person being appraised feels safe and relaxed, in order to get the best out of the appraisal interview.

The preparation we have done with them will have established some of the trusting relationship we need, to make the appraisal interview useful. However, we still need to make sure they feel that we are 'on their side'. The actual interview often brings out more anxiety and more formality on both sides.

We establish trust in a variety of ways:

- make the environment comfortable and relaxed; also ensure that the interview takes place somewhere where you cannot be overheard, and will not be interrupted
- greet them by name, in a friendly manner (the first impression always has an impact)
- make a little 'small talk' before you start straight into the interview; it reminds you that you are both ordinary human beings, not just appraiser and appraisee

- remind the appraisee of the purpose of the appraisal interview, and the structure; this sets the tone, and reminds you both that you are working together to achieve a useful end result
- state explicitly that anything said or discussed within the interview is just between you and them; if anything is raised which requires discussion with a third party, then you need to agree with them how that will be done
- check that your body language matches what you are saying; we all know instinctively when someone is only saying what we want to hear

Remember that these ways of establishing trust are only the starting point. You need to follow them through in practice, so that the person being appraised knows that they are genuine.

This means:

- don't allow interruptions
- greet that person in a friendly manner at times other than the appraisal interview
- take a few minutes to chat to them in the workplace as well
- make sure the whole interview fulfils its purpose
- maintain confidentiality
- remember to keep yourself open and positive

We none of us trust someone who turns their demonstration of trustworthiness off and on with us. We are suspicious of them if they suddenly become positive and supportive in a particular situation, and don't believe that it is genuine.

Establishing trust is a continuous process, not just a set of behaviours to be 'switched on' for appraisal.

Finding out

An important part of what you need to do as appraiser is to gather useful information from the appraisee. Once you have established some trust, they are more likely to give you genuine information, rather than say what they think you want to hear.

For an appraisal to be useful, you need to be very clear about the appraisee's view of things, what makes *them* feel they've achieved or progressed, where *they* think they need help, or improvement. All too often we impose our own view. Although the other person may go along with us, it rarely results in the effect we want, because it's not quite the same as their view, so they are less committed to it.

'To be complimented for excellent completion of my administrative tasks may be nice, but why wasn't my representation at the regional meeting noticed?'

'To have suggested that a counselling skills course may be useful is accurate, but right now I'd prefer to improve my computing skills.'

We have asked the appraisee to prepare by bringing examples of their own. It is vital that we give value to that preparation, and use it as the starting point for the appraisal.

We need first to find out what they have prepared. Simple questions are required here:

'What do you think are your achievements?'

Then we need to ensure that we have really understood what their example means to them. Our normal task would be to ask why that is an achievement. This is less useful than the following questions:

'In what way do you see that as an achievement?'

'What specifically makes you feel that is an achievement?'

We then have both the example and the opinion of the individual. We can now give appropriate recognition.

Notice that at first, an individual may only give one or two examples, and we may need to prompt them for more. Questions such as:

*'**What else** do you think of as an achievement?'*

*'**How else** have you progressed?'*

will tempt them into giving more examples.

In the same vein, we can find out what they think their obstacles to progress are.

'What do you think is stopping you progressing?'

'And what else?'

Finally, we want to find out what *they* think would enable them to progress and develop. We may have our own ideas, but theirs need to be explored first. We all prefer to implement our own solutions. So we need to ask questions like:

'How would you change this?'

'What do you think would help you to overcome this?'

'What would help you to develop this?'

Notice the common themes of these questions. They all start with 'what' or 'how' and they all ask the person to express their own view – 'what do you think . . .'

There may be information which you have which suggests something different from what they say.

- you may have something else which you consider to be improvement or progress; you can now add that to their own list, so it is a bonus, not a replacement
- you may have other areas of concern; you need to explain how they are a concern, how they relate to business or personal targets, and again ask the interviewee for their opinion, and their ideas of how to deal with it

> • you may have different proposals for development or next targets; you can now suggest yours, as additional possibilities – however, what is finally agreed will be from the choice of their ideas and yours, not exclusively yours.

It is often the case that the appraisee covers all the ground you have thought of, and sometimes more. If they are allowed to tell you, rather than you tell them, they are far more likely to act on it.

You are the reinforcer, recogniser, supporter and helper, rather than the dictator.

Listening

In order to find out someone's viewpoint effectively, we need to listen with full attention. This means that we listen, not just to what they say, but also to how they say it.

- Do they sound confident or doubting?
- Are they hesitating or in full throttle?
- Does their body language match what they are saying?

Listening with full attention means listening with our ears, our eyes, our hearts and our intuition.

And when you notice something which doesn't quite fit, ask about it. Possible questions might be:

'You seem unsure/pleased/worried/certain about that. What makes you that way?'

'How does that affect you?'

We can often save ourselves a lot of time and energy by listening with full attention. It helps us to spot quickly what is important in the communication.

Moreover, being a good listener is a quality which others really appreciate, and it helps to enhance the relationship.

Empowering

We want the person being appraised to take on more and more responsibility for their own development. For this to happen, they need to feel empowered to do so.

Empowerment has three main components:

1 reinforcing and encouraging the taking on of
  responsibility
2 giving clear and useful information
3 valuing the person's own thoughts, opinions and
  suggestions

Much of what we have described so far has this effect:

- giving them a clear purpose and framework for the
  appraisal
- asking them to prepare clear guidelines
- taking their preparation and examples first, before
  offering your own

All the time, we need to bear in mind that we want them to
decide for themselves, rather than impose decisions on
them. So you need to give them a lot of encouragement in
the first place.

Statements which start with the following are useful:

'I think it's excellent that you. . .'

'I like the way you . . .'

'I'm pleased that you . . .'

'I'm impressed that you . . .'

We often think these things, even say them to other people,
but don't remember to say them to the person concerned!

However, don't make such remarks unless they are genuine,
otherwise the person may feel that you are trying to con
them.

The interview, I: reviewing achievement

Today we shall begin to explore the structure of the appraisal interview and the context for fulfilling your role. Key points are:

- agreeing overall agenda and outcomes
- agreeing achievement and progress

Agreeing overall agenda and outcomes

In a formal business meeting, we usually have an agenda. We often forget to set an agenda for other meetings.

It helps to have something which gives a framework to the appraisal interview, and also links in to the amount of time available for it. This will enable you both to keep on track, and stay focused.

Appraisal Agenda

9.30   Review of previous appraisal and agreed action therein

9.45   Discussion of general progress and achievements

10.00 Identification and discussion of organisational issues

10.15 Identification of areas for further development or support

10.35 Coffee break

10.50 Agreement of an action plan

11.15 Recording of agreed outcomes and new targets

Confirmation of date for next appraisal

Equipped with a plan of this kind, having greeted the person being appraised, we can start by agreeing the agenda with them.

It is also well worth explicitly agreeing with them the outcomes you both want from the interview. These might be such things as:

- that both feel it has been a constructive meeting
- that recognition has been given to achievement and progress
- that realistic targets have been agreed, with appropriate action to be undertaken on both sides

Agreeing achievement and progress

The first stage of any appraisal is the recognition of achievement and progress.

Referring to targets
We have two ways of focusing on this area, depending on whether this is a first or repeated appraisal. In the latter case, we start by referring to targets set in the previous appraisal.

We might ask:

'What progress do you feel you have made against the targets agreed last time?'

'What examples/evidence can you mention to support this?'

We can then broaden the base beyond these targets to ask:

'In what other areas do you think you have progressed?'

'What else do you feel you have achieved?'

It is then appropriate to give due recognition for their examples, and add any further examples you have collected.

It can be helpful to ask a further question, to get some sense of their priorities:

'Which of these are you most proud of/pleased with?'

As they give you this information, remember to:

- ensure that you have understood fully their example/ evidence
- give value/recognition to their examples/evidence
- add to their list where you can, or certainly endorse it from your own information-gathering
- encourage them to link achievements and progress to both business and personal objectives

In this part of the process, you will need to begin to record the examples. However, beware: we often get so caught up in writing notes, that we don't give the appraisee our full attention.

It may be useful to have some scrap paper, and say to the person being appraised that you are just going to jot down a key word or phrase to remind you both of the achievement and progress covered.

Then, when you have covered all the areas of achievement and progress, use your notes to review them, and agree what should be written on the appraisal record. Completing it there and then, and showing it to the interviewee, also helps to build trust. A by-product is that it saves time afterwards.

Initial appraisal
On an initial appraisal, there are no previous targets to review. What is more, the interview often takes place soon after someone has started in their job, and they may feel that they have no significant achievement or progress to report.

We need to remember that this appraisal will set the tone for subsequent ones.

So, make sure you:

- go through the same preparatory process with the person
- ask them to produce their evidence, but give them the freedom to bring evidence from previous employment or other life experience as well
- do start with achievements and progress as the first area to focus on, and give recognition
- add in the achievement of getting the job, and settling in

What if someone doesn't feel they have progressed or achieved anything?
Do try to find some areas of progress. Sometimes people have very high expectations of themselves, and we can help them to recognise steps taken towards what they want to achieve, which they have dismissed as 'not enough'.

What if you don't think someone has progressed or achieved anything?
Again, do try to find something which can genuinely be seen as progress, as in the case above.

Are you expecting too much? As much as we can, we want to recognise achievement and progress, however small it may be. We then have something to build on for the next targets.

We all know how awful it feels to have failed utterly. That is not a good point from which to start looking at how to improve. At the very least, everyone can learn something from a failure; it's the first step forward.

Only as a last resort are we going to agree with someone that they have achieved nothing and made no progress. And if that happens, we need to question ourselves as well. How could we let that happen, and have done nothing about it until now?

Dealing constructively with lack of achievement

Having established some recognition for progress and achievement, we now need to deal with the second area of focus: where someone hasn't achieved or progressed.

Referring to targets
Again, we start by reviewing the targets set at the last appraisal, to discover if there are any which have not been met.

We need to be careful with our questions about a lack of achievement. It is very easy to make someone defensive, despite our best intentions. They already will feel disappointed themselves, so we need to be constructive with them, to help them find ways of overcoming it.

Useful questions might be:

- What targets have you not achieved?
- What have you achieved towards those targets?
- What stopped you from achieving them?
- What would help you to achieve them now?

Having listened carefully to the responses, we can:

- endorse any progress towards targets, however small
- add further suggestions for what might help

Often, people will blame the organisation, or other people. They feel they have become a 'victim of circumstance'.

There is usually some degree of truth in this, and it is important to take account of it. You may be able to help make a difference, say by agreeing to a change of priorities in the job description, and telling their supervisor. Or you may agree with them that the recent increased workload made the target unrealistic.

However, it is important to help them to identify some means of taking hold of the situation for themselves, so that they feel empowered rather than victimised.

Maybe they could talk directly to the colleague who is constantly interrupting them with queries. Maybe they could reorganise their workload themselves to give some regular time to a particular target area.

The question to ask, if they are feeling powerless to change the situation, is:

'And what can you do to help yourself to achieve this?'

Remember the result you want from this appraisal interview: a member of staff who feels valued for what they have achieved, capable of continuing to improve, and motivated to work on their own continuing development.

We want to reinforce their own ability to make a difference, not their failure to do so.

We may need to work with them for a while in the area of constructive ways of dealing with a lack of achievement.

Most of us are knocked back by failure, and become either defensive or helpless. We need to help our staff to feel safe in admitting to a failure, and positive about looking at alternatives.

It can be useful to remind someone that, as a small child trying to walk, they didn't say 'It's not fair', or give up, if they fell on their bottoms. They just got up and tried again, often in a different way, with more support from the furniture, until they could walk easily. The same principle applies to any personal development.

Different approaches you might use
1   *If their intended achievement or target was a large 'chunk'.*

An example might be: I want to revise all of my admin procedures, but I've only started on one or two.

Help them to break the target down into more realistic steps which they can achieve. Separate out the different parts which need revision, or stages of revision.

2   *If their intended achievement target was too vaguely expressed.*

An example might be: I want to improve my relations with other staff, but it's not really working.

Help them to make it more specific: with whom and in what way, and how will they know when they have?

3   *If they are lacking the confidence to get started.*

An example might be: I want to express my opinions at staff meetings, but I feel nervous of looking stupid.

Talk through with them what kinds of things they might want to express an opinion about, such as items on a staff meeting agenda. Ask them what they would like to say and how, so they have 'rehearsed' it. Offer them your support and encouragement to do it at the next meeting.

4   *If they have a specific difficulty.*

An example might be: I want to learn word processing, and I started the evening class, but then missed four sessions because of illness in the family, and I can't catch up.

Explore with them possible ways past the difficulty, and look at alternatives with them. In this instance options might include extra lessons, a different learning route, such as Open Learning, help from a colleague, etc.

Our intention is always to help them learn and move on from a lack of achievement or progress. As we continue to deal with the individual's feeling of failure in this constructive way, they will:

- be more honest about talking about their lack of achievement
- begin to be more constructive themselves in finding ways to have another go

Going beyond targets
So far, we have focused on lack of achievement or progress against targets. There may, however, be other areas where someone feels that their achievement or progress has been blocked. It is important to open up the discussion on these, because they are likely to be significant to the individual. You may use the question:

'Is there any other area in which you feel you have not progressed as you would have liked?'

We can then use the same approach as for those areas identified against targets.

What if you think there are other areas where there is a lack of achievement or progress?
If the appraisee has identified relatively few, then it may be useful to add in a couple. Make sure in each case that you explain very clearly in what way you consider there to be a

lack of progress, and be careful not to expect too much of the individual.

It is important to weigh up how important your identified areas are to the business. We want to maintain wherever possible an emphasis on the positive and constructive. Could these areas be used as part of the appraisee's general development plan, rather than used to highlight a lack of progress?

What if someone thinks they have no areas where there is a lack of achievement or progress?
We want to set the tone of continuous improvement, so we can delight in the lack of gaps and, at the same time, look for areas for development, which is much more positive. We might ask:

'In which areas of your work would you like to develop further? How?'

Initial appraisal
Obviously, in an initial appraisal, there can be no lack of progress or achievement.

We can therefore go straight to the positive tone of development, as set out above. This reminds both manager and newcomer that part of the purpose of appraisal will always be to encourage continuous improvement.

Recording the interview
While discussing this part of the appraisal, it is again important to make brief notes of areas raised and possible action to take.

These can be summarised and recorded, with the agreement of the person being appraised.

The interview, II: looking ahead

Today we will look at the last part of the appraisal interview procedure and how to conduct it. We will cover:

- continuous improvement and development
- setting goals and targets
- action planning
- finishing the interview

Continuous improvement and development

Let us pick up this theme from yesterday, and expand on it a little.

All too often an appraisal seems to say either: 'You've done all right, keep going,' or 'You're not good enough, do better.'

Successful appraisals say: 'You've got this far. Now where are you going?' They emphasise development rather than pick up on remedial needs.

When we look at ways of encouraging continuous improvement, we can take it through three stages:

1 improvements which will make it easier for the person concerned to perform well in their job – *job-related*
2 improvements which will enable the person to contribute even more effectively to business objectives – *company-related*
3 improvements which will develop the person's potential – *person-related*

In the first stage, we are encouraging the individual to look at ways of achieving their peak performance in the specific job which they have.

In the second stage, we are encouraging the individual to develop and demonstrate their potential for wider application. This may also help us to identify potential for promotion or new job roles.

In the third stage, we are encouraging the individual to 'round out' and develop their personal qualities. This of course, will also benefit them and the company in their work roles.

With these three possible areas for development, no one can say, 'There's nowhere further for me to go.' None of us have finished our development in any of the three and between them they open up a wide range of possible needs and wants in development.

We want all our staff to be constantly looking for what else and what more they can develop in themselves. This leads not just to successful appraisals, but also to successful organisations.

Setting goals and targets

To encourage this process of continuous improvement, we need to ensure that the person being appraised sets themselves appropriate goals and targets.

These emerge naturally from the previous sections of the appraisal interview on achievement and progress, areas of difficulty, and desired developments.

It is helpful to structure the formulating of the goals and targets, so that they are usable.

What are goals and targets?
A *goal* is the end result that a person wants to achieve.

Examples are:

- a further qualification in their subject area
- no work backlog
- more effective staff meetings

The problem with most goals is that they are fairly large, and often not very clearly defined.

It is important to clarify how you will know if you have achieved the goal, so that you can clarify what exactly it means.

Questions to help you do this might be:

'What evidence will you have that you have achieved your goal?'

'How will you know when you have achieved your goal?'

'What exactly will demonstrate that you have achieved your goal?'

After answering one of these questions, our previous examples of goals would be much clearer:

'I want to improve my skills in my work by taking a further qualification.'

'I want to improve my time management, so that I clear my work to deadline or before. I also want to tackle my present backlog until it is cleared.'

'I want my staff meetings to be shorter and to be fully attended. I want my staff to act on decisions made at the meetings.'

A simple way of getting these fuller statements of goals is to ask people to express them in this format:

'I want to improve . . . The result(s) will be . . .'

Targets are the steps along the way to achieving a goal.

Examples are:

- I will enrol in the college course
- I will timetable my work for the week
- I will ask my staff what they think would improve the effectiveness of our staff meetings

Targets need to be kept to a realistic size, so that they are achievable. They also help us to break down the achievement of a goal into small chunks, and to identify exactly what is required of us to achieve that goal. They are the actions we need to take.

To clarify the targets, we might ask:

'What do you need to do to achieve that goal?'

'How will you work towards that goal?'

'What is the first/next step you need to take to achieve that goal?'

It is important to make the targets specific, and where possible, date their completion.

So our examples might become:

'I will enrol in the college course at Smith College by 6th September.'

'I will plan out next week's work in my diary, with blocks of time for different activities.'

'I will put together a simple questionnaire on different aspects of staff meetings to use with my staff by next Friday.'

Now we have something concrete to do, rather than an intention. And we can produce a simple formula to help ourselves and others to set targets:

'I will do . . . by . . . in this way . . .'

Enabling others to set goals and targets
In the appraisal interview, setting goals and targets is the stage where we begin to pin down the wide-ranging review of past achievements and progress and newly identified areas for development. We want to turn this broad spectrum into a useful and managcable plan for the future.

We have, by this stage, notes on all the areas which have been covered so far by the interview. These notes comprise most of the 'menu' for possible goals and targets. First, they cover all the areas which are seen as important; the individual is far more likely to commit to further development in these areas. Secondly, they cover areas that the interviewee hasn't mentioned, but which we have already noted as important.

The only part of the menu not yet identified is anything which relates to changed or changing business or personal objectives.

For example, if the individual is about to move into a newly formed staff team with different responsibilities, this may throw up some different areas for development, which require goals and targets.

We can usually put all these elements into three areas of goals and targets to consider:

> 1 those based on a desire for development in areas of progress and achievement
> 2 those based on need for development in areas where there is a lack of progress or achievement
> 3 those based on a desire or need for development to accommodate coming changes

If you have been thorough in the review so far, you may well find that there are a lot of items which could potentially be the subjects of goals and targets.

It is vital that we find a way of narrowing these down to an achievable level. Better to set a limited number of goals and targets, and encourage people to go beyond them, than to cover every area, and leave them with so much to achieve that they give up.

How do we do this?

1   Sort out the possible goal with the person
Ideally, there would be between three and six goals.

Encourage them to choose their own. If you need to insist on a goal which they are not choosing, then negotiate with them.

For example, if someone is resisting becoming computer literate, and it is important for business objectives that they do take this on, then you may suggest that they take this as one goal, but also agree to their preferred goal of being more active in meetings.

Notice that sometimes the goals will still be the same as at the last appraisal. Someone may be working towards a large goal over quite a long period of time.

2   *Set up targets within each goal area*
Using the formula described above, we can help the individual to sort out their targets, which will be the steps towards the goal.

Again, we need to ensure that these targets are realistically sized chunks, which will help them to notice progress as well as achievement.

If they have not achieved a previous target, beware of setting exactly the same target again. We need to find out what stopped them, and if possible think of an alternative target. We don't want people simply to repeat a failure.

Action planning

Now we know what the person is wanting to work on during the period before the next appraisal, we need to help them to organise and prioritise those actions, to produce an action plan.

This is a vital part of the motivation of the person. Without it, it is easy to:

- be overwhelmed by the amount you have committed to, and put things off until the last minute
- avoid the areas you have less interest or motivation towards
- get so involved in one area of development that you go beyond your goals in that, but neglect the other areas

How do we action plan?

There are several possible strategies, but the most effective will have the following features:

- the action plan is clear and simple
- the action points will each have a deadline against them which spreads them across the period
- in each time period there will be some action points which are easy and pleasing to achieve
- major action points will be evenly distributed across the time periods

To achieve this sorting, it can be useful to use a simple matrix, to begin to classify the action points.

+   MUST   –

Must Want to	Needn't Want to
Must Don't want to	Don't need to Don't want to

WANT

NB If any point falls into the bottom right-hand box, then it is questionable whether it is a real target!

It is important to involve the person being appraised fully in the identification of categories for the action points.

From this, it is easy to put together an action plan which satisfies the effectiveness factors. The person themselves will usually do this part well on their own, if given the guidelines.

An example for a two-month period would be:

(M+W = Must+Want to, M = Must, W = Want to)

By the end of April

Find out about programmes on counselling available (M+W)

Produce a new format for monthly reports (M)

Read and pass on the professional magazines which are in my pending tray (W)

Reorganise the way I file things in my trays (W)

By the end of May

Meet with the training manager to sort out which counselling programme I can attend (M+W)

Introduce the new monthly report format to my staff with an cxample (M)

Clear three non-urgent items from my filing trays each week (W)

Check and renew the notice board (M+W)

The individual now has their action plan divided into manageable chunks. Targets are split into monthly targets, and each month contains a good mix of the simple and the complex, the important and the interesting.

Action plan for the appraiser

There may be items where *you* need to take some action. It is useful to note these down, and again put dates against them.

An example could be:

> **By the end of April**
>
> Inform the training manager of your support for the appraisee taking a counselling programme

Finishing the interview

It is important to remember to finish off the appraisal interview in a way which leaves you both feeling that it has been constructive and useful. The following points give you a framework for a satisfying conclusion:

1 Briefly summarise the process and reiterate your recognition of what has been achieved by the person, plus your support for their next targets.

2 Refer back to what you agreed you wanted as outcomes for the interview, and check that they have been met, on both sides.

3 Give the person a final opportunity to add in anything else they may want to say.

4 Ensure that you give a reminder in closing that you are both real people, not just appraiser and person being appraised – a simple reference, such as 'It's lunch-time now and I realise I'm hungry' or 'Look at that, it's pouring down out there!' is enough to bring back that fundamental reality.

5 Thank the individual for their preparation, participation and constructiveness; and wish them well with their targets. Remind them that if they get stuck with any of their targets, you are there to help if you can.

6 Agree with the person how and when they will be given their copy of the appraisal record, and the date and time of the next appraisal, if appropriate.

Completing the appraisal: after the interview

Today we will round off this guide to successful appraisals by looking at what follow-up we need to do to ensure that we have completed the full appraisal process. We shall cover:

- review of appraisal
- actions follow-up
- support systems
- ongoing appraisal

Review of appraisal

First we need to review the appraisal interview, to confirm for ourselves where it worked well and to identify how it could be improved.

This is most simply achieved by answering for ourselves some review questions. Examples would be:

- To what extent did we achieve the results/outcomes I wanted?
- What contributed to the success of the interview?
- What would have made it easier/even better?
- In what ways was the process of the interview effective?
- How else might I have made it even more effective?
- What are the key points I have learnt from this interview to help me to improve the next one?

By reviewing each appraisal interview in this way, we are practising what we are preaching to those being appraised: continuous improvement.

We are learning from the experience of conducting appraisals, so that we can fine-tune the overall guidelines to elicit the most effective results for us and for the interviewee. This continual fine-tuning is what produces excellence in conducting appraisals. It only takes a few minutes to conduct this review, and the results are well worth it.

Actions follow-up

In the course of the appraisal interview, you may have identified certain actions which you have agreed to take. It is important to follow up on these as soon as possible after the appraisal, while they are fresh in your mind and have some priority for you. It is all too easy to be 'overtaken by events' once you have finished the interview, and to forget to take the actions.

So we need to:

- action as much as possible immediately
- record in our diaries when we will action the rest

If nothing else, we need to make sure that the appraisal record is complete, that the person being appraised has a copy, and that our copy is properly filed.

Both the review and the actions follow-up require that you set aside an extra 15 to 30 minutes at the end of an appraisal interview, in order to complete the process.

Support systems

So far we have dealt specifically with setting up an appraisal framework, and establishing a process for successful appraisal interviews.

However, if the approach is to be fully effective, it needs to be put into the everyday work context of the individual. If we want someone to take responsibility for their own development, and to commit to targets which will enable that development, we must ensure that the relevant support systems are in place.

1 Other managers

In many organisations, staff may well be dealing with more than just their own line manager. It is important that others who may play a part in their development process are informed of the intention, goals and targets in that development.

These other people need to be enrolled into supporting the developments, so that the individual who has been appraised is not blocked by a lack of awareness on their part. This could be undertaken by the individual themselves, but your supporting advocacy will also be important.

Examples might be telling the training manager that you have agreed to a particular type of training programme for this individual; or asking the manager of another department to encourage this person to speak out in the working party which he/she leads.

2 Other staff

Sometimes the action steps we have agreed with someone will have some effect on others in the department or organisation.

Again, we need to ensure that we give our direct endorsement and support in effecting any changes necessary, so that the person appraised knows that our support goes beyond fine words at the interview and into practical backing.

3 Organisational systems and procedures

There is no point in agreeing with someone that they can work on adapting their recording system if the overall organisational system will not allow for a deviation from the standard.

Similarly, there is no point in agreeing with someone that they can put forward a proposal for a new discussion group, if there is no clear organisational procedure for doing so.

We need to ensure that organisational systems and procedures are flexible enough to accommodate any development plans the individual has.

We also need to ensure that those systems and procedures are known to the individual. Just because we know how they work, we shouldn't assume everyone else does.

Ongoing appraisal

There is one area of continuing support which we haven't covered yet.

However motivated the person may be when they leave the appraisal interview, they now have to maintain that motivation in the midst of the pressures of everyday work and routine.

For an appraisal to be truly successful, they will need some form of 'moral support' to keep them going for their targets. It is not enough for any of us to receive a 'one-off' boost, however positive and useful it may be. It may be six months, or even a year before the next boost, so how can we maintain the person's motivation between times? Two things can be especially effective.

1   We need to offer some continuing thread between one appraisal interview and the next
The way in which we do this may range from a formal arrangement through to something much more unstructured. What matters is that we demonstrate a continuing interest in and support of that individual.

Appraisal means according value, as a continuous process. People are not objects which don't usually change and can therefore be appraised just the once. People change and develop and therefore deserve continuous reassessment. What is more, the continuous reappraisal encourages and motivates them to continue to change and develop.

This may sound onerous, but you don't need to follow through by increasing the number of in-depth appraisal interviews. It is simply a matter of noticing and giving recognition to some elements of that person's development, and we can do that in a sentence in passing: 'I notice that you're enrolled on that programme – good for you!'

We also need to ensure that they know we are available to offer help if they are feeling stuck, and the offer of this help at the interview stage needs to be followed through in practice.

If someone says to you, 'I need a word with you. I'm still not getting anywhere in meetings,' then you need either to give them time there and then, or to arrange a definite time to see them and talk about it. Then they will know that the offer of support and help was genuine.

Some managers may prefer to structure this support, by putting in review times in between appraisals. This formalises the opportunity to recognise progress and to offer help on areas of difficulty.

2   *We may need to identify some form of mentor*
We may, as managers, be too busy to be the reference point for all our staff in their continuing development. Rather than feel guilty because we can't offer the level of support and encouragement we would like, we can identify, with the individual concerned, someone who could fulfil that role for them.

When this is done formally, we call this person a mentor. However, it can also be set up informally. We simply identify with the individual a person whom they feel would be appropriate and useful in encouraging them to sustain their development. It may be another manager, a supervisor, a member of personnel department or a colleague.

We then talk with that person about taking on that support role with the individual.

Most people choose well when consulted, and most people are pleased to have been chosen.

Conducting successful appraisals

We have now covered all the factors which can make a difference to the effectiveness of your appraisals.

When we go through all the different aspects of a successful appraisal, it can look like a daunting task!

So where do we start on improving our appraisals?

We can use the same principles and model for our own improvement as we do for enabling others to develop. Ask yourself: When I look at the full appraisal process:

- Which parts do I already do well?
- Which parts do I really want to develop?
- Which parts would it be most useful to develop?

From the answers to the second and third of these questions, establish goals and targets, and start to action them.

Remember that some of the recommendations in this guide may require some investment of time in the first place, but will save you time in the long run.

Remember that appraisals are successful when you have a clear intention in mind: to enable this individual to aim for and achieve their optimum.

Remember, above all, that you are dealing with a human being just like you. How would you like to be appraised? It's the simplest guide of all!

NOTES

N O T E S

Further *Successful Business in a Week* **titles all at £6.99.** A complete listing of all titles can be obtained from Katie Ingram on 0171 873 6261.

All Hodder & Stoughton books are available from your local bookshop or can be ordered direct from the publisher. Just tick the titles you want and fill in the form below. Prices and availability subject to change without notice.

To: Hodder & Stoughton Ltd, Cash Sales Department, Bookpoint, 39 Milton Park, Abingdon, Oxon, OX14 4TD. If you have a credit card you may order by telephone – 01235 400414.

E-mail address: orders@bookpoint.co.uk

Please enclose a cheque or postal order made payable to Bookpoint Ltd to the value of the cover price and allow the following for postage and packaging:

UK & BFPO: £1.00 for the first book, 50p for the second book and 30p for each additional book ordered up to a maximum charge of £3.00.

OVERSEAS & EIRE: £2.00 for the first book, £1.00 for the second book and 50p for each additional book.

Name: ....

Address: ....

....

If you would prefer to pay by credit card, please complete:

Please debit my Visa/Mastercard/Diner's Card/American Express (delete as appropriate) card no:

❑❑❑❑ ❑❑❑❑ ❑❑❑❑ ❑❑❑❑

Signature .... Expiry Date ....